The Best Manager™

Getting Better Results WITH People

By Craig Nathanson

Author of "How to Find the RIGHT Work during Challenging Times: A new approach to your life and work after 40."

The Vocational Coach
P.O. Box 6283
Petaluma, CA 94953
Phone 707-775-4020
Fax 866-279-5544
craig@thevocationalcoach.com

Layout and design: Natasha Nathanson
Editing: Natasha Nathanson
Proofreading and Layout: Natasha Nathanson
Illustrator: Kateryna Wert, Nastia Baskakova
Technical design: Gregory Banks

Nathanson, Craig, 1956 –
      The Best Manager / Craig Nathanson

ISBN 978-0-557-54927-6

    1. Management 2. Leadership 3. Business

Dedication

This book is dedicated to those managers which I have had the pleasure of working with. The good managers were more interested in people they managed, than the work itself. And really bad managers were operating as robots in a factory and related to the people they managed as just machines for getting the job done. I learned equally from both sides.

Table of Contents

Introduction

Sadly, the world now is experiencing the worst economic crisis in many years. While much of the blame has been placed on financial greed, corruption, and other related topics, I place the blame on poor management. The knee jerk reaction by most organizations has been to lay-off thousands of people, who were considered valuable when first hired. If history is any measure, many of these same positions will be hired back a year later at twice of the price.

This book is a reaction to the management crisis. As a result of poor management education, broken organizational systems, and an overemphasis on reward and punishment, today's modern managers are held hostage by the systems, under which they manage.

The only hope is for a new enlightenment by these same managers or better education for new managers. This book is an attempt to give useful, practical, simple, but effective tools and methods for great management.

Management is both an art and a science. Good managers care about the development of the people they manage as well as the development of the organizations they manage. They also know how to get the most important things done. The key to avoid the next management crisis is to educate and develop better managers. *The BEST Manager*™ *Getting Better Results WITH People* will give practical and useful ideas for those new managers just starting out, those in school studying management, and, of course, for those current managers who just need some fresh new ideas.

Craig Nathanson, May 2010

WHAT CAUSES MANAGEMENT PROBLEMS AT WORK?

Anything but a system

Many management systems are anything but a system. These organizations are a collection of people, habits, different behaviors, and expectations. Management is driven largely by external behavior (The bigger boss) and motivation (One's own). At work you often find too much competition between people, which gets in the way of productive teamwork and collaboration.

What causes the disconnect

Often it comes down to a confusion around what is expected. Many managers don't take time to clearly communicate the desired state of a program or set of goals. In many cases, these same managers have their own managers who are not clear either. The problem is often systemic.

The management system these days is fast

Managers often get caught in a spiral of competing requirements and demands. The BEST managers are able to deal with this effectively. They don't take things personally, and they are able to step back in the heat of the moment and look at the big picture.

Do you want to be the Best Manager?

This is actually an important question to answer. Some people enjoy doing their work through others. Some people like to get the work done by themselves. First, decide what work fits you the best. You can not be successful at both. Management requires the ability to be in many ways an excellent traffic cop. It is about always directing, keeping momentum and energy flowing, resolving problems, and keeping emotions under control.

One way to approach the role of management

Learn to accept change! The world of work is about change. Great managers are able to accept change and lots of it. It is best to come to work daily expecting change and in fact thriving in it. When there is no change in organizational life, the entire system starts to die slowly. Creativity goes away, motivation is low, and the environment loses all momentum.

Collaboration or competition?

The Best Managers enable their people to be creative, challenge the status quo, and encourage collaboration . Are you encouraging collaboration or competition? On one hand, people are told to work together, and yet they are ranked and rated against each other. This encourages a culture of survival of the fitest. While some might argue this is OK, I would say these cultures destroy morale over time and cause severe burn-out in the workplace.

Lack of self-awareness

Another factor which leads to a poor management is lack of self-awareness. When people come to work, they bring all their baggage from home. They bring their concerns together with the ability to get ahead, to be heard, and to contribute. The work anxiety is greater for people who have not gotten to know themselves at a deep level. The Best managers need to have a strong sense of who they are, what is most important, and how their most important values align with their work. Without this, it is difficult to be open, receptive, and caring to others. Worst, when there is a crisis, which is often at work, these same managers become prison guards and not leaders for their people.

The Best Managers align organizational mission, values, and behavior

So many organizations make a big deal out of mission statements and then fail to communicate the meaning of these statements. Worse, there is little of an attempt to define and align organizational values around the mission. The Best Managers take time to clearly communicate the organizational mission, organizational values, and how they align. Without this, there is often no consistency between groups and between managers.

The Best Managers align their own values with the organizational

The Best Managers believe in and promote the direction of the organization. Also, it is important to ensure that their own values align with the organizational. It is easy to tell which managers lead with passion and which simply lead as robots. Their people can quickly tell the difference!

The Best Managers share their strategies and plans

It is important to explain carefully the reasons *why* the organizational strategies and plans have certain directions. I have observed that people can figure out *how* if they know *why*. Too often managers give directions without reasoning what influenced the decision in the first place. When people feel like their managers don't share with them strategies, they leave their hearts at home and just drag their bodies to work.

Have teaching sessions

To be a strong manager, one must be comfortable with teaching. There are many opportunities to teach during the day as problems come up. Like children, adults need to understand mistakes that were made and possible better choices for next time. Poor managers rely on punishment and threat, which only leads to more bad behavior out of fear.

Improving the organization takes work

It is often amazing to me how organizations and their leaders take serious actions to improve their products and equipment for producing these products, but they do very little to develop those people who are doing the main work. The Best Managers help people to improve their work. This can only occur through mutual support and understanding. Also, strong managers meet often with their people. I used to have a simple process. I would meet bi-weekly with each staff member. I used to give them the first 30 minutes to discuss whatever they wanted to discuss. Then, in my turn, I would ask a question: "With regards to your work, what do you want to do more of, less of, and how I can help?" This process gave me much leverage.

Management is about leverage

Getting the best results with people is hard work. It takes patience, strong and frequent communications, and empathy in many cases. The biggest organizational problems can be solved by doing simple things over and over. This will go a long way towards resolving management problems at work. It will also enable people to be better followers and better leaders.

Learning summary and next steps

Become more self-aware. Have more empathy towards others. Set clear expectations for people and be clear with all communications. Be a good teacher! Use opportunities at work to role model what is expected and turn work activities into an ongoing classroom.

GREED, MONEY, AND ITS AFFECT ON MANAGING

The problem with greed

If to take a look at economic problems in the past years, one will see the impact of greed on the economic system. Nowadays it seems enough is not enough. The organizational drive to increase margins, lower costs, improve productivity continues to be the main emphasis in business. After all, this is what our schools teach. What gets lost is the balance between the drive for just making money and making work enjoyable. When people find joy in their work, they want to help to improve the business and they are more creative and willing to offer suggestions. While the desire by management is for collaboration, often the management does the opposite placing people in competition one vs. another. This leads to mistrust between employees and management.

Greed takes over

Soon people start to compete in the race for the increasing salaries and awards. At the end, the winners feel more pressure to stay on top, and the losers feel like well losers! To improve the teamwork, the emphasis should be on the collaboration and not on competition.
I have seen so many performance systems that were set in January and frozen until the following December. As business environment changes, managers need to work together with

their staff to change goals and objectives. In many organizations, performance goals are established early by top management and, as a result, these goals and the possibility of reward becomes the only thing which people are focused on. When the performance system is tied directly to specific goals with no flexibility, greed takes over, short-cuts are made, integrity is compromised, and ethics disappear.

Why people dislike their work?

People grow to dislike their work for 3 main reasons: the work no longer aligns with their abilities and interests; the environment no longer enables them to grow and develop; the management is poor and not supportive.

Often managers forget that motivation at work is complex and driven by a number of factors. Often those silly contests, performance goals, and motivational lunches produce the opposite of the desired effect.

Many HR programs, for example, aim to get employees motivated by external factors as the better review, the holiday party, and the annual bonus. Better would be to offer education to help people learn how to motivate themselves, which in return would produce more productivity and joy at work. Just once, I would like to see a performance review which measures the amount of joy at work. When people love their work the organization benefits in many ways. Creativity is high, communication is open, and people take risks.

The Best Managers know that it is hard to expect long term success when the only motivational strategy is external rewards.

Don't reward, especially with money

What would an organization do if they couldn't reward with money? I often ask this question and always amazed with the blank looks I receive...

There are many ways.

First give people work worth doing. Put a process in place to help match people to the right work. There are many people in the organization that may have strong skills but are no longer interested in work they are doing. Find new levels of work for them. There are also people in the organization who are very interested in aspects of the business but lack the skills. Give them new learning opportunities.

When people enjoy their work, it becomes the reward itself, especially for the older worker. Provide opportunities for self-assessment, group collaboration, and risk taking without penalty for failure. This would be more helpful than offering bonuses for achieving new goals. The carrot and stick approach has not done anyone a favor.

The problem with ranking, rating, and competition

Many firms cherish their annual ranking and rating systems competing workers against one another. It drives away creativity, joy, and passion for workers. This approach may work in short term for the younger worker but not for the more experienced worker over 40.

Why should this matter to the organization? Despite the economic crisis, there are still more work related choices than ever before. People can still choose to leave and go elsewhere. Only the most successful firms will thrive with people who stay for a long period of time.

Organizations that put their employees against one another will find this strategy inadequate for the long term.

We need to put emphasis on people

The Best Managers know how to balance achieving work results and enabling people to find joy in their work. The Best Managers demonstrate that they care about their people despite their performance. The Best Managers know that people don't wake up in the morning to do a bad job. The Best Managers step back and study the overall system always seeking to make improvements where needed.

Place emphasis on the team

Often at work, we have challenges and are not sure what to do. In other cases, we feel unchallenged but with many skills. Placing the emphasis on teamwork ensures a culture of working together, helping, teaching, and leading. Teams solve problems better than individuals. This can occur only when the system promotes collaboration vs. competition. The Best Managers reward teams and encourage more collaboration.

The management system must change

Many management systems based on either behaviorism by B.F. Skinner or Scientific management by Frederick Taylor are outdated and need to be changed. People today have more choices about what to do and where to do their work. Society itself has become more mature in the last 100 years. People are growing to expect more out of their work than just a paycheck and a bonus. The Best Managers provide outlets for creativity, innovation, and autonomy.

Make collaboration the goal

When people are encouraged to work with one another, fear tends to disappear in the environment and productivity can increase. With collaboration, people become more aware of the interdependency with others. Also, they are more interested in results of their combined work.

Make actual work to be a reward!

As people feel joy at work, this becomes a reward. The Best Managers work hard to stay out of the way as much as possible.

Eliminate fear and threat

Adults don't respond well to threats and when it repeats on a regular basis they start to sabotage the system undermining the aim for quality results.

Time for a change and new approach

The era of greed is over. We need a new era of the Best Managers who try new approaches to enable people to have joy and meaning at work WHILE also getting great business results!

Learning summary and next steps

Focus on people development. Focus on people development over profit. While this might seem risky, the bottom line is that profit will actually increase over time. Enable people to find joy in their work by aligning their abilities and interests. Minimize reward and emphasize giving people work worth doing. Be a role model focusing more on teamwork and less on competition.

TREATING PEOPLE AS COMMODITIES

The culture treats people as commodities

I see it everywhere - people working in jobs which carry little meaning and provide little support for personal development. Worst, the culture treats people as commodities. Performance review systems, manager-employee meetings, and even rewards are set based only on recent performance. The recent performance is everything that matters. As a result, people feel like they are treading water in their jobs.

Lack of support for people development at work

Part of it starts at the top of the organization. If the leader values people development, then the organization will place a high priority on education and new opportunities. But, unfortunately, people development is not an organizational priority and is left up to individuals to find their own ways. The Best Managers encourage their people to take risks and give them developmental opportunities at work.

What happens when people development is ignored in the organization?

People drag themselves to work only for the money. This is another extreme from doing voluntary work. Creativity goes down, motivation goes down, and spirit at work goes down too. Unfortunately, the bottom line is seldom measured against the amount of joy the workers have at work; however, it is a very real factor to pay attention to. When people feel joy and happiness at work, they will go an extra mile to offer suggestions for improvement. When people feel they can take risks at work without the fear of punishment, they will try new approaches, implement new ideas, and everyone will benefit from this.

The Best Managers always have people development as a key priority. This impacts team assignments, new role opportunities, and educational opportunities at work.

What does people development really mean?

I would take this to the extreme. For example, years ago I had an employee whose husband had just passed away. I knew she liked to work in her garden. When she returned to work, I paid for her to attend a one day inexpensive class on gardening. This had nothing to do with her job as an IT technician, but it had everything to do with her development. She came back refreshed and appreciative of the opportunity to learn something new, which she was deeply passionate about. Did this help her productivity at work? Yes, and, in fact, it helped to ease her transition back into work after a difficult time in her life. Of course, later other employees wanted their own one day class, which I also accommodated as one-time exception.

The Best Managers know that sometimes doing an extra effort towards employee development will provide great leverage for management. Too many organizations have silly rules that only allow education for job related topics. This narrow interpretation prevents people from exploring new areas and new ways of thinking. The rules based manager will protest and suggest that the organization should not fund education (they call this training) that does not directly relate to the job. This is the usual short term thinking that contributes to why so many people separate their work and the rest of their life. Encouraging traditional and a blend of non-traditional education will encourage intellectual growth, creativity, and actual loyalty to the organization over the long term. This is something that will impact in a positive way the bottom line of any organization.

How do you implement a personal development program at work?

I can tell you the way not to do it! Don't give people a checklist form which has three columns: Development opportunity, Class, and Date. This approach will guarantee the opposite effect. People will feel pressure to sign up for a class, managers will feel pressure to assess, and the results will seem like a performance review.

A better way

Personal development starts with a personal plan. The Best Manager encourages each person to make a list of his or her abilities (things the person is able to do if motivated) and interests (deep interests). The next step is to have the employee align the areas that match. This is where the development should focus. The development should focus around a combination of education, new work opportunities, and self-study. What if a person's matrix of interests does not align with his or her current work? The Best Manager will encourage a frank discussion of how to get closer to the work this person really wants to do. In some cases, this can be a creative exercise to find a better position in the organization. In other cases, it can be an opportunity to develop a plan over time to move the person out of the company which is best for everyone involved.

Motivation should come from inside

Just because a person has a competitive salary, nice office, and two-week vacation doesn't mean at all that he or she will be motivated. This is a very personal issue. To get to the root of motivation requires communication between the manager and an employee around what is most important. Sadly, managers jump to conclusions around poor performance, and, as a result, people start to feel like commodities as they are sorted, ranked, rated, and judged. It is very similar to the work B.F. Skinner did with animals in the cage watching which one would find the lever to raise and escape from the cage. The same happens to the person who has been labeled as a poor performer at work and, thus, placed under a performance improvement plan. Once in the plan (or in the cage) a person will do anything to escape and improve his or her condition. This is only short term and in the long run harms motivation and interest in the organization.
The Best Managers always look at performance from a systemic view and seek to understand the reasons for behavior and motivation. The Best Managers help people learn how to motivate themselves.

We need better managers

During difficult times, people will always generate their own crisis and anxiety. The last thing people need during this time is further threats, rewards, punishments, and motivational programs to keep the spirit up. This all can increase instability. The Best Managers, instead, focus on better utilization, better communication, and better planning with their people.

Learning summary and next steps

Match people development and organizational goals as they do go together! Enable people to craft their own development plans. Realize that you can't motivate others, but you can teach others how to motivate themselves!

THE BEST EDUCATION FOR MANAGERS

Crisis in management education

There is no consistency today in the way we educate managers. Larger organizations tend to have more comprehensive programs. If we look at the business results of the past year, it will show that these programs have not been very successful. In the US over 99.9% of all organizations have less than 500 workers. Many of these organizations have little to non-existent management education. There is a great opportunity now to improve. Most of the big companies use the traditional approach. Their managers are given a combination of classroom education, role plays, and outside experts with their theories. In many cases, there is little follow up and measurement around the results of the education.

What does the Best Management education look like?

The Best Management education consists of a combination of classroom discussions and real life practice. While some background theory is important, it is better to have discussions around management practices and different approaches. The problem with traditional management education is that it is standardized and designed to fit all employees at once. For example, a new manager is having attendance issues with one employee. The traditional advice is to warn the employee that his behavior will lead to punishment if not corrected. Another example, managers are given exercises in class to try their skills at giving tough messages to make believe employees. Managers learn the right way and the wrong way, and the training is complete. Unfortunately, correcting human behavior is more complex.

Management is both an art and a science

Socrates had it right when he said asking questions was the best strategy to lead people to where you wanted them to go. Management education should be focused around discussing many possible solutions and strategies that might be different for each situation. Most HR policies tend to use the same rules for all people, but people are different and have many different issues, and managers must learn how to approach each person in a unique way. I had an employee once who was always late. My peer manager suggested that I should punish this person, but I took a different approach. I sat down with this person one to one and showed empathy. After asking many questions, I discovered that this person was caring for ailing parents at home and his challenges were just overwhelming. We worked out a new schedule for him to come to work a little later in the morning and leave later in the evening. This gave enough time to take care of his parents until a nurse arrived. As a result, his productivity has soared, and there was never any problem again. Under a strict set of policies, this person would never have been given a second chance.

Invest time to educate employees about mission, values, and behaviors

Did you ever notice families with well behaved children who just seemed to know what to do at all the time? They seemed to behave very independent and almost too mature for their age. This was a result of good parenting, which, I suspect, was a combination of paying a lot of attention to the goals of the family, values, and expectations. At work adults are just like children but with bigger bodies. All adults require care, opportunities to thrive, and strong and open communications.

Empty mission statements

Many organizations invest time to place charts on walls describing what the organization stands for. However, they are missing the charts reflecting values of the organization and expected behaviors. The Best Managers invest time getting people to do more than just memorize the mission statements. The Best Management educational programs open the discussion why the mission statement is important and what the organizational values are. For example, if the organization says serving the customer is the most important value, there are countless definitions and examples of what this means. Finally, people are clearly given examples of what behaviors are expected to support the mission and values. In the above example, people are told that they are expected to make decisions at the lowest possible level using creativity when solving customer problems. This type of Best Management education makes work come alive for people.

Measure for development not for rewards and silly contests

The best way to destroy management education is to surround the activities with rewards and silly games. For example, I can remember one program that according to test results the managers who scored the highest were given dinner coupons. I can remember another program to give out candy and movie tickets in class for participation. The Best Management education activities are open to all employees and have follow up opportunities after class to manage!

Everyone can benefit from management education

Many organizations only offer their management education activities to their star performers and emerging leaders.
However, the best system gives opportunities to all people to go through management education. The BEST approach to the management education is to figure out a way and then process to enable all people to manage right after the education. In some cases, people will directly lead others. In other cases, people will lead projects. For the majority of people, they will be allowed to manage their own work free from micro-management, limited decision making ability, and free from the threat of punishment and the promise of reward.
The Best Management education is a creative and inspiring process not an event. Just one look at the collapse of the US economy is alarming enough to know that the past management practices at the global level have led us down a path of destruction and reduced quality of life. Now is the time for new management models and practices.

It starts with new ways of education and understanding what it means to be the Best Manager!

Learning summary and next steps

Make the education open for all employees. Give opportunities for people to rotate assignments, try out new roles, and gain deeper experience in areas which they want to learn. As a result, the organization will benefit and have more vested people at work.

OVEREMPHASIS ON REWARD AND PUNISHMENT

Employee recognition

Does this sound familiar? It's Friday and another day at the office. Today is an employee recognition day. As usual once a month the department manager gathers the whole group for one hour meeting. Employees come to the faceless conference room and await the monthly employee recognition celebration. A committee of managers and a human resources representative meet monthly to decide which employees to choose for the award. The group selects 5 people around some subjective criteria and the award winners are announced in this team meeting. Each winner gets a $50.00 coupon for dinner. As the names are announced, everyone in the audience shifts uneasy in their seats hoping their name won't be called. The winners feel a little embarrassed to be picked and wonder if this will affect their relationships with their peers who didn't get selected. They also worry if they will have to work even harder next month. The meeting ends with a cake and all in all around 2 hours of productivity are lost, which accounts for thousands of dollars. After that management and human resources go away feeling good that they motivated the staff!

It is not possible to motivate others

It is not possible to motivate others; yet, we still try. Managers assume that implementing programs to motivate with the promise of reward or the threat of punishment is just what people need to stay alert at work. From my experience it's quite opposite. More emphasis should be done on teaching people how to motivate themselves, which in turn leads to greater productivity and overall benefits to the bottom line.

More emphasis on alignment of abilities and interests

People feel good at work when they can align their abilities and interests. People feel even better without the threat of punishment or reward. Managers should hold off the temptation to reward or punish. They both work only short-term. As the British researcher Herzberg suggested, most people want the same basics at work (good boss, nice office, competitive salary, and interesting work). When this is in place, people are more interested in their own personal growth and at some level making coherence out of the work they do.

I can remember early in my work career a sales contest. The manager brought all of us into a room and told us how poorly one product was doing. He announced that the person who would sell the most in the following month would win a trip to Hawaii. I can remember thinking to myself, how silly this was. I figured even then that this contest would actually drive down sales. The overemphasis on the prize would cause loosing the focus on the customer. I was right. Sales dropped

30% the following month during the contest. It would have been better to explain to the sales team the problem with the underperforming product. Also, it would have been better to work on improvement of the product, so that the sales staff would be proud to sell it to the customers.

The famous Chinese philosopher Lao-Tzu said, "It is better not to make merit a matter of reward, less people conspire and contend."

The danger of quick results

Modern management likes quick results. Placing emphasis on reward and punishment is easy to measure. It can scare people enough to get short-term results. In a long term, it robs the soul out of people and their work. There are many dangers with rewards. When reward is the goal, the focus gets very narrow.
I can remember my senior management days when our bonus targets were set in January. We reviewed our goals monthly to make sure our large bonus numbers could be met. When the bonus can be up to 10 times of your base salary, this can be a huge incentive. The problem with this that as the business requirements change, the management still remains focused on the bonus goals from earlier in the year. Instead, would be much more important to focus on the work which needs to be done now, as the business changes.

Rewards lead to bad habits

When rewards are at stake, people will only focus on achieving of the reward and nothing less. When this occurs, courage, creativity, and risk taking go down.

Studies by Deci and Kohn and others have even suggested that at best by rewarding people who don't like their work, they get satisfied only until the next bonus. Worst, when rewarding people who like work, their performances go down with the new threat of monitoring for an activity that they enjoy doing.

The aim is collaboration

Ask any manager and you will hear, "We want our people to work together". Yet, if you study the management system, you will find processes, programs, and reward activities that force competition among people.

Stop the overemphasis on rewards and punishment

Stop the overemphasis on rewards and punishment. Pay people competitive salaries and provide work worth doing. Help people to do right work which gives challenge and matches their abilities and interests. Where possible, give employment security, eliminate unnecessary forms of competition between people, and encourage open communication and trusting environment at work.

Throw out old ideas

The time is now for new approaches to enabling success at work. Think, if you had to enable people development at work and you couldn't reward or punish, what would you do? This is the most important question for the Best Manager to ask.

Learning summary and next steps

As a manager, think about what you would do to enable people development and feedback at work without the promise of reward or the threat of punishment. People will appreciate and look forward to their work without gimmicks and contests to urge them to work harder. As a result, people will feel vested working in an organization which honors people and values differences.

BAD VS. GOOD PEOPLE

Labels at work

It can be easy for a manager to label people as bad or good performers. This performance labeling tends to be a convenient way to quickly categorize people. It is efficient for human resources. Once labeled, people can be given promotions or demotions, merit or punitive action, more money or less money. Management and Human Resources can now implement programs of the month such as succession planning, employee of the month, and so on. This approach seems to have come from the behavioral management theories of the past. These ideas do nicely align with short-term thinking and the idea for quick results at any expense.

The danger of labeling people

Having been labeled, people will tend to perform to the level of management's expectation and no more. Those labeled as good performers will tend to have extra anxiety to keep up with manager's expectations. Those who labeled as poor performers will find it difficult to do better under the threat of having to improve. For better management, it is wise to avoid this approach.

A better approach

It is a far better approach to look at each person as unique and different. This can be demonstrated through regular development reviews, plans, and ongoing focus on employee development. It is better to invest time and meet on a regular basis with all employees. Establish regular meetings focused on development. Make it an agenda for employees to discuss what they want to do more of, less of, and areas which they are finding difficulty with. Make these development sessions focused on the positive development of each person. Under this approach all people will perform better having their manager show interest and support in their development. Of course, performance ratings and reviews are necessary in evaluating the annual performance, but these should not be separated from the developmental discussion. It is common that the developmental discussion rarely occurs as part of the annual review event. Make employee development an ongoing process. This brings great management leverage and both employee and organizational improvement.

Organizational behavior and labeling

There is a tendency in many organizations to rank, rate, and sort people against one another. They produce quickly a list of good people and bad people. The problem with management tool is that it is mostly subjective and people can be labeled unfairly. Employees lose out on new opportunities to contribute once their managers had labeled them in negative terms. In many cases, just the opposite may be true. Being a better manager, step back from a system view when having difficulty with an employee and ask a few questions. Does the person have the tools to be successful? Is there something in the environment that is preventing success? Is there something can be done to remove barriers and assist? This mindset will go further towards helping people to succeed at work.

Is there a good employee and a bad employee anyway?

Poor performance at work can be attributed to many things. The most common from what I have observed is either the person was a wrong fit in the current role, or the culture is unhealthy in the company. This can be the result of poor management.

The danger of ranking and rating

Many firms, especially Hi-tech companies, have adopted the ranking and rating model of employees, which is effective only in a short term. Any management process that is purely subjective is bound to cause tension. Better to include people in their own evaluations and next steps. Management can help people to make better contribution to the organization through two way communications, ongoing feedback, and more focus on collaboration vs. competition.

Look at each employee as an asset and not as a commodity

The Best Manager looks at all people as assets. The Best Manager is always thinking of where to use people matching their high challenges and high skills considering the needs of the business. When people are viewed as assets, the manager looks proactively how people can be used better. This system gives flexibility for more job rotation, for more cross functional assignments and more feedback. When people are viewed as JUST a commodity the system tends to be more one way directional. People start feeling being used and not appreciated.

Better ideas to replace labeling

Establish a database of abilities and interests of your people. Combine this database with business needs and employee development plans. As new opportunities come up, utilize the database to assist in selecting people for assignments. This helps people to feel vested in the business and less constrained by a job description. This leads to more risk taking and creativity which is a good thing for the organization.

Encourage movement throughout the organization

The Best Manager encourages employees to move from assignment to assignment or job to job despite past performance. Many people become stagnant when they are forced to remain in the same position year after year. Sales people are told they can't go into marketing, engineers are told they can't go into sales, and human resources staff have difficulty moving into business line functions. Moving people around the organization spreads knowledge and enhances learning.

What occurs when people feel included and valued?

The Best Manager knows that when people feel valued at work, they get more done, have better relationships with their peers, and make the culture stronger. When people feel like they are viewed as unique and not labeled or forced to compete against their peers, motivation can increase, the organization and the employees benefit, and the Best Managers just get better!

Learning summary and next steps

Treat people as owners of the organization and as professionals. Adults will appreciate this. Eliminate the games of having people compete vs. one another. Communicate often asking for ideas and feedback. Give people an opportunity to contribute to the areas that they are most interested in.

Remember, when people feel good about where they work, they provide better customer service and better productivity!

MANAGEMENT AS A SYSTEM

What is a management system?

A management system has many processes on multiple levels. Some of them are important, some are not so important. Those processes have a start and a stop, an in and an out. A process can be mature and working well or can be embryonic and very immature. A process can be broken if some pieces are not working well together. The system then represents the state of all of its processes. The idea of a system is to focus on long term stability. Understanding the system helps to avoid making short-term decisions that may temporarily fix the immediate need but damage the system in the long term. It is easier to focus on cause and effect when trying to resolve problems. For example, it is very important to understand what process is used to evaluate people. If people are evaluated in a way which encourages competition among peers, this will influence the overall competition and affects the climate in a company in an unhealthy way. If people are encouraged to work together on teams and collaborate, the system will look different. In this case, people will tend to help each other more without fear of sharing information which might affect their performance ranking. The way managers communicate affects the overall system. If management typically keeps its doors closed and rarely shares business updates with the entire staff, the system will tend to operate in a way which encourages secrets, gossips, and many other problems. If management keeps the doors open, it will help open communication and overall sharing of all business related information to all levels. In this type of system one will see more risk taking, creativity, and interest in the business by employees.

The Worst management system

The worst management system encourages limited information sharing, a lack of creativity, unfairness, and less opportunity to contribute and participate in the overall business. I will give you a few examples of bad management systems.

A top manager asks human resources to establish a ranking and rating system among the staff as an effort to improve performance. However, instead of positive effect, this leads to less teamwork, impacts the relationships in a bad way, and deteriorates the bottom line.

Another manager might establish a new policy that limits working overtime. Instead of positive changes, this leads to the increased amount of errors in the workplace as employees rush to complete their work, because they don't want to work long hours without being paid.

A manager in another company implements a new policy, which restricts employees from transferring to new positions if they are not performing well in their current role. This leads to people leaving the organization for lack of opportunities. Now the manager will have to hire replacements which hit the budget.

Another manager decides that the first cost cutting activity should be to eliminate free coffee and instant soup in the lunch rooms. This does not lead to much cost savings but instead sends a message to employees that they are not that important. Thus, it leads to work slowdown, poor morale, and people leaving, which ends up costing the organization many times over what the coffee and instant soup cost!

These are examples of behavior which is usually well intended but simply not thought through from a systemic view.

The impact of non-systemic thinking in management

Short-term and non-systemic thinking leads to decreasing revenue and morale, worsen working relationships, plus, overall causes fear and lack of trust. A recent county government manager decided to shut down many local parks just to resolve a short-term budget gap. As a result, those people who used to pay on weekends to attend these parks now traveled to new areas in different counties where they spent their weekend money. This could have been avoided with systematic thinking upfront. The way management position itself will influence the system and the behavior in it. Just wander into any retail store and you will notice the health of the system. For example, there is one office chain I used to visit where overtime became more difficult to find any employees working there. It seems in this store they are each given assignments in the morning having to do with store maintenance. As a result, in the system there is little focus on the customer. Overtime, customers will visit competitors and much more is lost in this system.

On the other hand, I can think of a local bagel shop I visited where the employees greet me by name and remember my usual order. I notice how happy all employees seem. Later I learned every employee has been given a share of the business and is considered as an owner. In this example they don't hide from customers as this is their business. I am sure you can now think of similar examples.

Non-systemic thinking leads to entropy, errors, and a general decline of the business. The Best Manager thinks through all decisions and policies and in advance determines the resulting impact on the system.

The best management systems

The best management systems are aligned and interdependent. All processes make sense and impact each other in a positive way. There is a favorite grocery of mine, which I like to go. All employees are treated fairly and equally. No tasks are too big or too small for any employee. Since people are treated well, they are motivated to contribute their best at work. This store pays the highest in its industry with the best benefits. There is job rotation so everyone gets to know all aspects of the business. Communication is frequent, there are no closed doors, and the managers are also accessible. The best management systems make sense. The people who work in these systems know what to do, have complete autonomy, and confident that they are treated with respect. Each business process leads to another. If a customer requests a product which the store does not have, this product is ordered and now the inventory process and related processes adapt to this customer request. Employees are given updates on new products coming in and old products going out. This constant flow of open communication leads again to employees feeling vested in the business.

In the best management systems, people can explain how things work and why. The business works well, employees are happy, customers feel good about the service, and the brand builds a healthy reputation. Most important, the business thrives and grows.

How to implement a good management system

Think from a big picture view, identify the most important processes, and examine how this processes work with each other. Try to understand which processes have the biggest influence on the organizational goals. Put people in charge of these processes to improve them. Have open feedback and communication at all levels of the system. Encourage risk taking, creativity, and personal development.

How to make a good management system last

Make the people who work there the most important, more important than customers, more important than profit. People will rise to the occasion helping to build a system which lasts.

Involve all levels of staff including them in all major decisions and actions. Enable staff to feel like owners of the business and they will work to improve the system. As a result, everyone benefits.

Why systemic thinking matters?

Without systemic thinking, the same issues go unresolved. Time and resources are wasted and customers and employees are unhappy. Systemic thinking leads to the improvement of all working parts. With systemic thinking, processes become mature, people make better decisions, and the organization, its products, and services thrive. This is the BEST management!

Learning summary and next steps

Take time to make a list of the most important processes in the organization as defined by which impact the most objectives. Assign people to own, measure, and develop these processes. Before making decisions, think through how other parts of the system will be impacted. Ask for input often, be always open to change. As a result, people and the organization will get more flexible and get better results.

THE IMPORTANCE OF SELF-AWARENESS

What is self-awareness?

This is unknown territory for many. In school we are seldom taught to do deep reflection. As we get older and become adults we get caught in the cycle of productivity and consumption. As a result, self-reflection becomes something to be avoided so as not to slow oneself down. Self-awareness means knowing yourself at a deep level. This includes as Jung suggested the shadow side which is everything in us that is unconscious, repressed, undeveloped, and denied.

Without this deep awareness of who we are, these ignored feelings can surface in actions later and cause conflicts. Deep awareness includes understanding ourselves. No one is perfect, and a deep understanding of ourselves, our fears, the things which excite us can all help us to live in the greater world and in harmony with others. Self-awareness also includes the basics such as being clear about what we like to do and what we don't like. It can include feelings about events and how they impacted and changed us. Self-awareness means to understand and feel comfortable with your own behavior.

What does self-awareness have to do with management?

A manager's day is filled with lots of change and decision making. Many of these decisions include people. Every move by a manager has the potential to have a big impact on others. The self-aware manager understands this and thinks through decisions and communications with others before acting. The self-aware manager tends to be calmer, have more empathy, and able to think through challenges much better. The self-aware manager is able to think from the other's perspective which helps in people relationships, communications, and decision making.

The effect of the self-aware manager

First, the self-aware manager is more confident and knows that nobody is perfect and yet with self-awareness comes the confidence to make decisions and communicate their intentions to others. For people who work for a self-aware manager, there is more joy at work. Those people feel listened to, treated fairly, and in general they have a role model of personal development. It is critical responsibility for a manager teaching people about importance of self-development and self-motivation.

The danger of avoiding self-reflection

We can see this daily in many organizations. Decisions made without consulting others, autocratic leadership policies aimed to catch people doing the wrong thing, and other related aspects of theory x managers (assuming if left alone people will do bad things). The result is a culture of poor morale, limited creative thinking, and risk taking. All of the above can bring down an organization and impact the bottom line.

The importance of self-awareness in the organization

When managers are demonstrating self-awareness the whole organization takes on a similar behavior. People invest more time to get to know themselves. The organization offers personal development education and encourages growth and development. Customers get better service with employees who are more confident and more aware about who they are and what they do.

When the organization supports personal growth and self-awareness, the overall group tends to help one another more. People tend to show more care towards others, conflict at work is decreased, and overall people get along better.

Important questions to ask to become more self-aware

Ask yourself these questions: Who am I? What do I love to do? Which fears do I have about my life and what can I do about it? Who do I love in my life and why? What things give me the most joy? What activities cause me the most anxiety and what can I do about it? What is most important to me and how do I follow what is most important? Lastly, what goals can I put in motion to align to what is most important?

The payback to better decision making

Self-aware managers make better decisions. Why? They tend to be more reflective and take more time to think through implications of their actions. Self-aware managers think more from a systemic view. They understand how their decisions and behavior impact the whole system and others.

The payback to society

The self-aware manager contributes more to society through actions and being a role model. Society over time benefits the most. Programs and strategies for building society take into account human factors and implications. There is more emphasis on understanding all parts and how they make up the whole system. This type of thinking impacts decisions, strategies, and where we place our focus and effort.

Learning summary and next steps

Take time for self-assessment. Understand yourself on a deeper level. Think through your behavior on a daily basis. Make sure your behavior is aligned with your values and what is most important to you. When your work aligns your abilities and your interests and you have deep interest towards it, your life will feel more congruent. As a result, you will have more time for those who you manage and more empathy and understanding towards others.

WHY MOTIVATING OTHERS DOESN'T WORK

Incorrect starting point

Almost everywhere you turn, you meet another rewards based incentive program to motivate people. This approach can work short term only for people who don't like their work. But as time goes by, these people will only demand larger rewards to gain the same satisfaction. And for people who actually enjoy their work, their performance and motivation will most likely decrease in short and long term since they are the ones who don't require external factors to do what they enjoy. I have found that the best way to ensure that people are at their best is to align their abilities (what they are able to do if motivated) and their interests. The intersection is where people will thrive.

The problems with motivational programs

Each person is unique and has different needs. Most motivational programs assume that all people are motivated by the same factors. This is simply not true. Why in many motivational programs there are different winners and losers? Whether it is the sales trip to Hawaii, the employee of the month parking spot, or the employee of the week free lunch, these programs only offer the opportunity for the unhappy workers. These programs are in use because they are easy to implement, measure, and produce. They don't take deep thought or long directions to understand. Do this and you will be rewarded or do this and you will be punished. People are much more complex than that.

How not to motivate people

In order to learn more about how to motivate people, first, learn how NOT to motivate people. Here are a few ideas. Give people work not worth doing or which does not add value. Micro-manage people by giving them less opportunity for autonomy and decision making freedom. Make people compete against one another or against standards. Use this as the sole guide for rewards and punishments. Showcase the winners and losers to everyone else. For sure, this will help to lower morale and motivation. Focus on productivity and efficiency and not on personal development. Ignore to assess the abilities of people and interests and, instead, cattle herd them ONLY to work which needs to be done in specific ways.

A better approach

It starts with the hiring process. Hire people who want to do the work you have available. Make people development a higher priority than profit. That's right, you read this correctly. When people feel like their life means something to those they work for, productivity will soar to all time highs and, of course, will be followed by profit. Give people full autonomy in their work. Let people make all decisions, work in ways which best suit them, and encourage collaboration but not competition at work.

Enabling motivation

Enabling motivation means teaching. Managers teach people how to motivate themselves and in turn people find ways for self-reward, praise, and internal motivation. Stop the silly Friday dress down days, employee of the month awards, and special parties for high performance. This rarely works for children so why to assume that this approach to motivate works for adults. Treat people at work as owners and, as a result, people will act and make decisions like owners.

New results for the Best Manager

It takes hard work for a person to be the Best Manager, especially when it comes to helping others to be motivated. The first step is to realize the difference between external motivation and enabling motivation from the inside. As a result, people and organization will thrive and work better together which can only help the bottom line.

Learning summary and next steps

Teach people how to motivate themselves from the inside out. Enable people to invest their time to gain greater personal self-awareness and personal insight. As a result, you will have a workforce which is more stable, consistent, and happy!

PLANNING AS A SYSTEM

Management as a planning system

When managing, it is important to understand the most important processes, which are required to meet business objectives, and then make necessary changes in planning. The management planning system has multiple important processes. They are divided between setting strategic and tactical plans, people development, and operational processes. Prior to establishing strategies, it is important to define an organizational vision and ensure that all employees understand the vision and have an opportunity to contribute towards it. This vision starts with a described end state. The Best Manager needs to explain what the organization will be like in 1-2 years or in the timeframe of the planning horizon. It is important for management to define other elements of this end state. For example, what will the customers say? What will the employees say? What goals do you expect to be achieved? This ensures that everyone on the team understands and works in the same direction towards implementation and development of the vision. Next is mission. It should describe what the organization does and how to help everyone understand the main purpose and objective of the organization.

Establish values

What is most important in the organizational environment? Organizational values should be clear, communicated, and demonstrated. For example, perhaps one of the organization values is customer service quality. This should be defined clearly. Managers must be a good role model of the organizational values. 3-5 values are quite enough, if defined clearly and people are able to follow.

Defined values might be around customer service, employee risk taking, creativity, working together, and so on. What are the expected behaviors in the organization? They should align nicely under each value. Behaviors aligned to core values, which are taught and demonstrated throughout the organization, give a powerful lesson and template for people to follow.

Do environmental analysis

Once the organization has defined the basic framework for how it will operate, then it is time to collect data for the planning process. This should be at a minimum an annual process to review but driven by routine processes throughout the year. It's important to collect organizational assumptions. What are the overall assumptions that will drive the planning activities that everyone can agree on? For example, the company will grow 10% in the next year, add 8 locations, and hire 67 people. It is assumed that the organization will phase out some old technology and bring in new technology. With clearly listed assumptions, management can make plans that make sense. Every plan must have customer input. In general organizational leaders find what they are doing well, measure it, and decide to do more of it. This is a backwards approach. First of all, managers should survey their customers and understand what is most important especially among products and services currently being offered. Then, managers should measure how the organization is performing according to what is important to the customer. This leads to the better planning system.

Explore customer trends

It's also important to look at customers, and their objectives. What services and or products do they appear to be using more of or less of? What other factors of customer behavior can be explained and written down to help the planning process? What kind of customers are fading out, buying less, and what customer base is growing? These questions should understand the reasons why? In any plan the external economy must be taken into consideration. Where is the growth, decline and why? How will new laws, policies, and external factors affect the organization? There should be a clear statement in the plan around the economy, and how it affects the organization in a positive or negative way.

Learn from your competitors

Who are the competitors of the organization? What do they do better or worse? What are the most important processes in the company needed to achieve organizational goals? For example, if your company exports shoes, then shipping is major process. A shoe manufacturer might review the process they use to ship shoes to distributors and compare this to how their competitors handle their shipping process? How do others outside of the industry handle shipping products to their distributors? How do other working well firms handle their relationships with their distributors? Once you take time doing this kind of research, it pays off later improving all processes in the organization and its planning system!

Now look inside

How are the skills of the current employee base matching up to the new plans? What skills are emerging and will require new educational plans and tools? What skills are declining and will require re-training for people to shift to new areas of higher return. Managers should create a database to understand the strengths and areas of interests of their people. This will help when the process of reviewing emerging and declining skills is underway. Matched with a database this enables a powerful knowledge resource about the most critical resource of the organization! It's important at this point of the plan to survey all people and understand their ideas, and what they feel is going right vs. wrong. The data should be available to everybody and, more importantly, the action steps and recommendations always visible. Following this overall process based on a planning approach, the budget can be set. Too many budgets get set prior to any planning and new goals are established without a clear basis. The budget should be set as a result of customer feedback, strategic direction, and available funding!

A nested planning system

The above enables the development of a companywide set of long-term, medium-term, and short-term strategies, which can be set and shared. Each plan element should have an owner and clear metrics should be established, which describe what the goal is, when it is expected, and what metrics will represent success? Managers should make sure as many people as possible contribute to the annual plans. Plan leaders should hold regular update meetings open to all employees. When people know both plans and status on a regular basis, it will open up communications and will enable people to feel more vested at work. At the same time, it will help to move plans forward.

When The Best Manager looks at the management planning process as a system, it helps to prevent decisions made without data and includes everyone in the process from customer to company leadership.

Learning summary and next steps

Management is a system and it is important to understand the fact that when a decision is made, the entire system gets affected. It is important to understand also what processes drive work in the organization. This leads to improving the planning system. In this process all possible data should get collected, and all team members should be involved. The organization can produce new objectives for the following plan period clearly defined with metrics and owners assigned. This should be a result of key customer input, which should have been collected around importance and performance. It is important for management to give visibility to progress through the year via operational reviews while making them a routine process. Finally, placing an emphasis on people development in the plan process will ensure that people are moving forward and in alignment with organizational plans. Management planning takes discipline, quality thinking, and involvement. As a result, the chances are greater that business goals will be achieved!

WHAT MAKES FOR A GOOD LEADER?

What is leadership?

Great leaders are creative, decisive, and charismatic. Strong leaders understand what is important to them. They are strong at persuading and communicating the vision which they want others to have. Great leaders display personal mastery and passion for what they lead. They encourage education of the team while keeping everyone moving towards a similar vision. Great leaders are systemic thinkers. They understand the implications of their decisions and actions on the overall system which they lead. Leadership is about creating and motivating the change which needs to occur.

Great leaders know how to manage their time. They continuously develop their personal skills. Great leaders know how to make others feel important. Think of a leader for whom you worked and who made you feel good. This is the affect great leaders have on others. Great leaders think about the affect of the decisions that they make. Great leaders are good at coaching, which tends to occur in private and demonstrate high integrity. Great leaders are often great communicators. They know where they stand with regards to performance and plans. Great leaders know how to celebrate team success and, as a result, build great teams in the process.

What are the different styles of leadership?

Different people behave differently in leadership positions. Perhaps you had a leader who was very fair and democratic. These types of leaders put an extra effort to ensure that people are well informed and are part of the team. At times, this type of a leader may even act as if he or she is in service to others. Leaders like this are values centered. They let everyone know that what they believe is most important either through their behavior or by what they say. Another type of leaders is more structural and task focused. These leaders focus on the task at hand. The way things are done is more important than the way people feel. And, there are leaders who are authoritative and perhaps political at times. What is most important to these leaders is that they are in charge, and their actions reflect how they will benefit most. In my experience people appreciate those leaders who show interest in others, communicate well, listen to their employee, and are willing to make changes based on input from each person.

Who are the great leaders?

There are many great leaders, and I have my favorites. I remember in the late 1990s meeting with Jeff Bezos at his Amazon headquarters in Seattle. In those days people were skeptical how far he could take his little online bookstore. While we met and discussed with his staff some partnership ideas, Bezos had an opinion about everything, and he was very good at explaining how all his ideas linked to the bigger vision of Amazon. Jeff Bezos was a teacher and extraordinary strategic thinker. Although his vision was big, he was also good at some little things, and operated in a very methodical way. Great leaders like Bezos are not afraid of making decisions, taking action, and learning by doing mistakes. I also think Mother Teresa was a great leader. She was a role model for doing what she loved. She never accepted limitations and never strayed from her mission of helping the poorest people of India. This is what a great leader must do, clearly define what you want to accomplish and never stray from the mission. Bill Gates, the founder of Microsoft, is also a great example of a leader. He combined vision, passion, and customer orientation to make the computer industry what it is today. Great leaders have passion and channel into worthy causes. Perhaps not as well known, Li Ka Shing, one of Asia's richest individuals, tells people that he never plans to retire and knows his priorities. He demonstrates high integrity in all his business dealings. These are important elements of strong leadership. Steve Jobs, founder of Apple Computer, blends a charismatic quality with vision and strong sales skills. Having a vision is important but being able to sell the vision to others is equally important. These leaders are great role models which you can follow to become a great leader of others too!

What is the difference between leading and managing?

Leaders provide vision and inspiration while helping to motivate others towards a common goal. Leaders are focused on creating and facilitating ideas and opinions from others. Strong leaders promote collaboration and not competition between members of the same team. Most of all, leaders sell tickets for the journey! Management is different. The same people should aim to be good at both but this is often difficult. Mangers need to focus on driving the bus. Strong managers should be focused on planning, organizing, and monitoring.

To manage requires subordinates. One can lead without necessarily having subordinates. Sometimes managers have a short-term view and need to be results oriented. When leadership and management go together, it is good for organizational success.

How to find new leaders?

First, let's look at three categories of leaders: those who perform well as leaders; those who don't; and those who want to be a leader someday.

Leaders from first category already lead people and enjoy what they do. In many cases great leaders have their abilities and interests aligned. The work they do fits their self-image and their role at work. For the second group of leaders, who are not doing well, the story may be different. It is possible that for this group, there may be a misalignment of challenges and personal skills. It is also possible that these leaders are just working under a broken system, which is impacting their ability to get anything done. Finally, this group just may have poor role models. This group needs coaching, education, and maybe re-evaluation to find out what is not working. They may need a change with support! Leaders from the third group, whom I call emerging leaders, are not leading today, but they are motivated to take on more leadership responsibility. This leaders need more opportunities, education, coaching, and some apprenticeship or transition time into new opportunities.

Make an inventory of the team. Identify the right combination of necessary skills. Identify strong leaders who have these skills aligned with their interests. Find out who wants to be a leader as not all people are interested in leading others. Finally, create new organizational opportunities for new leaders.

Learning summary and next steps

There are many models to become a great leader. It starts with the internal motivation to lead others, the knowledge for this, and the opportunity. Decide if you want to be a leader of others. Then, think about who you want to lead and why. Identify what new skills you need to acquire now to succeed. Take actions to move towards more leadership opportunities.

COMMUNICATION: THE ESSENCE OF ORGANIZATIONAL SUCCESS

Importance of communication

Failure in communication is the biggest problem of management. When this occurs, it affects everything. Overall performance of people decreases, goals are not clear, people build incorrect assumptions, and relationships at work suffer. Especially during challenging times, it's critical to be more effective when communicating. Employees want to know what is going on during times of change. This is when the breakdown usually occurs. Many managers fail to understand how important to communicate with integrity, openness, and on regular basis.

Communication is the exchange of messages between people. And, to make the communication effective is the most critical skill for managers. Good communication leads to personal power, motivation, resolving conflict, solid delegation, and smooth facilitation and collaboration among people. When communication is abrasive, insensitive, and poor, it leads to a breakdown in relationships. The organization becomes full of distrust and uncaring interpersonal relationships. This occurs in organizations where employees get new information about changes without knowing all the reasons why.

Importance of clear communication

The traditional model of business communication has been always focused on accuracy and efficiency. It is sort of like a conduit model containing three parts: a transmitter, receiver, and noise. It has been my observation that most interpersonal problems at work occurs due to problems in communication. Communication after all is a complex process.

Let's take Terry and her boss Ron as an example. Terry calls Ron and tells him, "I won't be able to work again tomorrow. This pregnancy keeps me nauseous and my doctor said that I should probably be reduced to part-time." Ron tells her, "Terry, this is the third time you have missed work and your appointments keep backing up all of us. We have to cover for you and this is messing up all of us."

This was an example of poor communication from both sides. Terri wanted to have more empathy from her boss Ron. But she encoded this message to make it more official to add an excuse for missing work. Ron is not really happy with Terry anyway and decoded this message as just another excuse from Terri. He was not clear either about his further plans about her.

You can see that the margin for error is quite high at each step in the process of communication. Some social psychologists estimate that there is a usual loss of 40-60% of the meaning in a message from sender to receiver!

Barriers for effective communication

There are many barriers for effective communication at work. The way we use the language because of our cultural and educational differences can lead to misunderstanding. Our perception of one another depends on many factors, what generation you belong to, what gender, where you grew up, what your beliefs are, and so on. Often, we don't know how to read body language, how to listen, how to react in a conflict situation in a professional way. Overall, lack of knowledge affects our communication at work.

It can be helpful to understand non-verbal cues

Some research suggests that we communicate non-verbally 70% of the time! It can be helpful to learn to read visual cues, how different people use their hands when speaking, and their tone of voice. Learn to make an eye contact depending on another person's culture. In North America eye contact preferably should be soft, so make sure you are not staring while communicating. For middle Eastern, the "eyes are the windows of the soul", and it is important to look at each other while communicating at all time. In Japan there is very little eye contact made. In North America our physical space is a big deal. For example, 2-4 feet is reserved for close friends and family, 4-12 feet is the best space for social communications, and 12 feet when giving presentations.

A good communicator has good listening skills

The Best Manager is a great listener. The Best Manager listens openly and with empathy. The Best Manager judges the content but not a person. The good listener uses many methods to listen and fights off distractions when listening. The Best Manager knows the art of asking good questions to gather data. The Best Manager responds with interest when communicating.

How to give a feedback

Many managers are reluctant to provide feedback but quick to evaluate. Many managers are afraid how their feedback might be received. They may have personal biases which affect their feedback. In giving feedback, The Best Manager should be descriptive to make sure the receiver gets a description and not an evaluation. Strong managers focus on the behavior and not on the person. It is better to say, "I don't like the way the project which you were on turned out." rather than to say, "I don't like your project". Even worse to say, "I don't like you!"

While we usually don't tell others at work that we don't like them it tends to come out in other ways.

Communication is more than just sending a message

While e-mail has made our communication more productive, it has also made it worse in many ways. How much time is wasted while a person on another end is either hiding behind an e-mail or did not even receive your e-mail because it ended up in the spam folder. At least, when you have a possibility to contact someone eye to eye, it is fairly clear how your message is received. When in doubt, communicate in person.

In buildings where offices and cubicles are next to each other, strong managers encourage people to get up and walk around to communicate. It has been my observation that the healthiest organizations are loud and active. You will see people standing on their chairs shouting over cubicle walls. The organizations in trouble are the ones where you can hear a pin drop when you walk in the halls. All what you hear is the sound of typing, people sending messages back and forth between their next-door cubicles. Management problems are many times is a failure to communicate. And as we have learned, communication is more than just sending the message!

Learning summary and next steps

Take time to learn and practice the art of communication to ensure the message you deliver will be received correctly. This takes discipline, patience, and a sincere interest in keeping positive communication and dialog flowing between people.

BUILDING BETTER TEAMS

Why many teams don't work well together

Have you ever thought why the team that you were on didn't work very well together?
Many teams originally were set up to fail. In sports, you build teams from individuals with best achievements. In business, we hear many times, the sports analogy applied but in most cases it couldn't be farther from reality. In business, teams are seldom picked and mixed together based on the best individuals and their skills. Typically, people wind up on a team based on a range of factors. They were on this team before and it was part of their job description. They were told they had to be on this team. They were added to the team as a reward or worse as a punishment! Usually, the leaders of these teams are only symbolic. They are called team leaders in many cases. They are responsible for the team but without real authority. They are also expected to perform their other full time jobs. These types of teams fail.

Build the right team

It is important to build the right team from the start. Take an inventory of the people in your organization. Compile a database based on interviews and surveys. Ask people, which types of roles they feel challenging but also they have the skills for? Which roles best align their abilities and their interests?

Find out who wants to lead and who wants to be leaded?
Ask people, which roles fit the image of the work they most want to do. Part of this inventory process is to understand from each person in the organization what they want to do more of, less of, and how management can assist. As a result of this process, you have a database which contains real input from people. Then, when the time comes to put together teams, you are able to review the database and select people who fit best. This is what the Best Manager does.

Encourage and support

Once the manager sets up a team, people spend time helping to set vision and clarify goals. Then, the team is free to self-manage and make process without micro-management. Teams are comprised of people, and they need support and encouragement but not threats, punishment, and rewards. People just want to feel like they are making a contribution. Successful teams go on to complete many winning projects if the upfront structure and ground rules are established.

Promote collaboration, not competition

The Best Manager treats all team members the same way and rewards them equally. The team knows its goals and desired state. The work itself becomes a reward. If the reward must be given, it should be equal to all members as a result of the team progress towards common goal. Making individuals on a team compete with one another is the way to conflicts. When, instead, people feel that everyone has the same goals and incentives, collaboration is more effective, productivity is higher, and accomplished results are much better.

Set a clear desired state

This is the most important first step for a team. The Best Manager spends several hours with the entire team communicating the desired state and taking time to ensure that all members understand clearly the vision and the path. Without a clear vision, team members will start distracting one another decreasing productivity, and the desired result will not be achieved.

Have better team meetings

Team meetings should be held in two different formats. There should be a regular operational meeting (process meeting) where people give updates and the leader also communicates status and next steps. This type of meeting should be rigor and structured. Teams also need a second type of meeting. These are mission meetings where the group is either to solve a problem or to create a solution. These meetings should be of a brainstorming type and run in a creative, collaborative way. Teams can break down when there is confusion about expected outcomes.

Rotate leadership

Rotating team leaders on a regular basis is healthy for the team. It also helps everyone to feel vested in the outcome. Plus, when you lead one day and follow another day, you gain new experience and gain new perspectives. Letting people take on leadership roles for the first time will help to build confidence and also be a valuable development activity at the same time. A well structured team will not let new leaders fail knowing that one day they will be asked to lead.

Learning summary and next steps

The Best Manager designs teams around people. It is an art of combining what they want to do and where their abilities and interests fit best. As a result, teams will be more successful and reach their desired states faster. As a first step, take an inventory of your team. Then, put together the next team based on the experience. You will see new results!

WHAT DOES QUALITY REALLY MEAN AT WORK?

A new definition of quality at work

While the traditional definitions and measurements of quality are worth aspiring to, I would like to offer an additional level of thinking. Webster's definition defines quality as a general term applicable to any trait or characteristic whether individual or generic. In management, quality depends on many factors. For example, being open and honest at work, seeking positive change, being proactive, and looking for new creative solutions can all be ways of seeking a quality direction. I would even suggest that taking risks and making mistakes can fall under quality seeking category if one's heart was in the right place. There is always much that is going on at work that was never explained or communicated. The Best Manager is open, honest, and seeking positive change. The Best Manager is communicating both the *why* and the *how to change*. This is quality and we need more of this from managers.

Examples of bad quality management

I can give many examples of bad quality management approaches. It can be: Picking a quota for how many good performers there should be vs. poor performers. Deciding that the goal for revenue growth this year should be 8 % based on no data. Deciding that only certain people are eligible for job transfer based on their past job performance. Continuing routine processes which adds no value and which people dislike such as the annual performance review, the employee of the month award, and the performance ranking and rating system.

The Best Manager is on the lookout for processes which no longer make sense and ready to be changed.

Examples of good quality management

The Best Manager holds creative brainstorming meetings seeking for new ideas. Customers and employees are invited. The Best Manager implements collaborative processes at work which enable people to work together and not compete vs. one another. Other examples of management quality would be giving people a voice at work. This includes scheduling team structure and communication methods. Having processes which encourage creativity, risk taking, and new approaches are all examples of good management quality. When in doubt, the Best Manager works on common solutions, listens well, and communicates through multiple methods.

How to encourage and demonstrate quality at work

The Best Manager doesn't settle for the status quo. The Best Manager is always seeking better ways to get results and new approaches to old problems which have not been tried before. The Best Manager isn't afraid to ask questions, challenge the status quo, and be creative in getting results with people. The Best Manager involves customers when seeking new approaches and when resolving difficult problems. All of this provides an open door for people to practice new ways of quality as well.

When quality is poor

When quality is poor, products and services suffer, morale is lowered, and customers lose confidence in the brand. It becomes harder to attract both new customers and new employees. It becomes harder to retain employees. As a result, people drag their bodies to work and leave their hearts and minds at home. No one cares any longer and everyone seems to go through the motions at work. Office gossips take over and productivity goes way down. The Best Manager is always on the lookout for poor quality and doesn't ignore or accept status quo.

When quality works!

When there is quality at work, people have more energy. As a result, new ideas seem to flow throughout the organization, people tend to be happier at work and enjoy the culture more, and also the brand and organization has a better reputation with its customers. Quality breeds quality. People start to look out for one another more, helping, teaching, seeking to improve. More people want to join the organization when quality is up and less people want to leave. The Best Manager is an example on a daily basis of quality in both actions and values.

The ways to measure quality

Make measurement objective. Ask how, why, how much, and

when you had examples of approaches in an environment which were role models of quality. The Best Manager measures with the team the important factors. People have their work measured as a collective process. Each person can see how his or her work fits into the bigger picture. There are opportunities to communicate and see how other projects and efforts throughout the organization are moving along. Decisions are made based on first understanding trends using data and input. The Best Manager knows that people respond better when they understand how they are being measured and for what.

No more contests

The Best Manager does not reward quality with silly games such as Friday dress down days, movie tickets, and free lunches. The Best Manager knows that providing external rewards only reinforce the need for bigger and better rewards next time. The Best Manager makes quality a part of the culture and behavior. As a result, there is no need to reward more than a manager would reward good listening skills.

Learning summary and next steps!

Make a list of ten processes in your organization which are not adding value. Make a second list how you might replace or delete these non-valued activities and show what the impact might be on people and the organization. This would be a good process to involve the whole team and would be a good way to role model positive management and everyday quality at work!

WHY TRADITIONAL CAREER DEVELOPMENT DOESN'T WORK

What is career development?

Many organizations view career development in a typical way that a person will move up over time within a specific job ladder. Compensation guidelines are established to enable growth within these ladders. The better idea of career development is to assist people to match what they are good at and interested in. The career development has to be a plan with a clear path to upward mobility and increased opportunities.

Typical organizational approaches to career development

Many organizations have established job ladders and training programs for career progression. The focus is growth within the company and usually within the specific job group. People who can move up the career ladder are usually limited by compensation schedules, performance reviews, and lack of opportunities. People with poor performance reviews are even more restricted. When career development programs remain limited to a select group of people, most will feel left out or maxed out when pondering career choices within the organization. Additionally, most career development programs are only focused on growth within the job group, and it can be difficult to move outside of one's core job. It is more difficult to get educational opportunities in new interest areas that don't relate to one's job or area in the organization. For example, many people who are burnt out in their current role might benefit from a job rotation to another area of the organization. A new learning process might improve the person's attitude towards the organization and the organization might benefit from a new perspective as well.

What happens during a poor economy?

The worst is how organizations deal with career development in a poor economy. Educational opportunities or training programs are cancelled, and development talks between employees and management are put on hold. The environment takes on a crisis mode, and things like career development are left for better times or at least that's the way it seems. The Best Manager knows that during challenging times even MORE emphasis should be focused on people development to keep morale high and more importantly show that the organization will invest in people on an ongoing basis despite the economy. These methods don't always cost money. For example, implementing coaching programs within the organization to focus on development, implementing new job rotation opportunities, and enabling people to offer education to peers on their areas of expertise are good ways to show people during difficult times that the emphasis is still on them.

The developmental life cycle and work

One might assume that people will always make good career development decisions; however, this does not take into account the dynamic aspects of the career making process. For example, as people age, they gain more experience, more self-appraisal, and, at times, more clarity about their work and life. Some may find that it is the time to reevaluate their life and career status. Some wonder how they would actually spend their day if they had unlimited flexibility and opportunity. As people age, they might be more receptive to change in their work. Just being presented with data may not be enough to offer guidance at this stage of life. This time, it can be critical for individuals to be aware of their needs and work towards satisfying them while at the same time accepting and reconciling past events, both successful and those which were not as successful. Again, this can require both self-reflection and opportunities for discussing with others work related options and possibilities. This inner reflection is important as it can lead to inner readiness for change and growth. The internal assessment can help to see the gap between where a person expected to be and the present state. This tension is inherent in the human condition and therefore critical for mental well-being.

New approaches are needed

Early in the career, many people carry out their work because they have to. Little thought is given to what work they would rather do. Over time, especially as people age, they discover that what they most want is a sense of fulfillment and coherence about their work. This insight is usually not thought through very deeply. It starts as a feeling that one's work is no longer fulfilling or satisfying. The career development process, which is only linked to existing job ladders and organizational opportunities, limits growth. New approaches are needed to encourage people to grow and develop. It can benefit both people and the organization. These approaches range from enabling all people to try out new roles, get education in new areas, and have formal processes in the organization for self-discovery and greater self-awareness.

The enlightened organization

The enlightened organization focuses on career development during good times and bad times. During bad times, they invest in people even more. The Best Manager knows that when people have opportunities to learn new things, which interest them and they can apply at work, joy and productivity both improve. The Best Manager understands the link between worker happiness and work output. The Best Manager knows the difference between just having job ladders vs. an ongoing process for education and opportunities for current roles as well as opportunities to re-invent or expand into new roles for people.

Learning summary and next steps

People thrive when they have opportunities to learn and develop into areas which deeply interest them. When people feel like the organization cares and supports career development during good and bad times, they respond with more energy, loyalty, and focus. Re-evaluate your career development activities in your organization. No matter if it is a one-time program or an ongoing process, it should be both unique to the individual and yet linked to the business objectives of the organization.

What new activities should be added and which ones should

be dropped? What are the emerging and declining skills in the organization over the next 12-24 months? What process can be put into place to match both needs of the organization and people needs with the goal to move towards greater joy and fulfillment at work? Just discussing this new approach will do wonders for morale.

ALIGNING INTEGRITY AND FINANCE (IT IS POSSIBLE)

The most common financial mistakes managers make

In many organizations managers are not taught how to manage their budgets. In some cases managers are given budget responsibility but not budget authority. In these organizations, it takes 5 levels of signatures to get a few hundred dollars approved. Worst, managers are given both responsibility and accountability but little financial training. As a result, budget forecasts are a guess and managers tend to spend whatever they have, because they are afraid if they don't, their next quarter budgets will be reduced. Revenue goals or plain budget goals are not based on data from customers or trends; they are simply numbers picked from the sky. If the organization grew 5% last year, then 10% would be a better goal for this year. The problem with financial projections starts when programs and projects get either overfunded or underfunded based on the initial projections which were not made with financial integrity.

What is financial integrity?

Financial integrity is having a system of budgeting and spending open, easy to understand, and based on data. Projections are based on real trends, real customer orders, and consistent with past earning and spending. When managers cover up budgets to hide either overspending or spending enough to justify next quarter's budget, integrity is compromised.

How to demonstrate financial integrity

The Best Managers plan and communicate spending in clear ways. People understand what decisions and assumptions guided financial decisions and spending. All employees have access to the financial progress in the organization, so they can contribute. Employees are given the opportunity to learn about preparing a budget, forecast, and related terms. With open communication, managers can be given responsibility and authority to approve or deny spending. Financial bureaucracy is reduced when people understand how money and spending flow in the organization.

Put new financial measures in place

During a financial crisis many times managers are focused on how to reduce spending. They are rarely given the opportunity to increase earning. The Best Manager puts key operational methods in place to ensure financial integrity. First, spending and earning trends are open and available to all employees. This helps people to feel vested and make better decisions. Second, there are regular operational reviews to discuss spending and earnings. The more managers know the more chances are that they can make better decisions with their spending. The Best Managers build budgets based on data and not guesses.

Educating the workforce

The Best Managers educate the workforce on finances. I knew one organization which offered a personal finance class for all employees. This helped to educate people about their own money so they would be more sensitive to the spending in organization too.

Telling the truth about money

Sadly, many public organizations today micro-manage their finances to tell the story which analysts, investors, and others want to hear. Many times numbers are manipulated, changed, modified to meet external projections and demands. As a result, it becomes more difficult to manage internal spending and earnings when the numbers get changed to meet the expectation of a specific audience.

The Best Manager is open and consistent with the spending and earning. As a result, people, who work to produce the revenue, have a stronger commitment to financial integrity.

Learning summary and next steps

What processes do you have in place to forecast and manage revenue and spending? Is it based on data and actual customer orders? Are these numbers simply made up as you go to meet targets and bonuses? What education can you put in place to educate better all employees on the finances of the organization? How can you give them financial education to help them improve their own finances and to help them to become more sensitive to the money flow at work? What financial review processes can you put into place so that all employees can become more aware of how the organization is doing with regards to spending and revenue?

HIRING AND LETTING GO

Why hire in the first place?

Any employer hires for the same reason, they have a problem which needs to be fixed. When hiring, the Best Manager looks at three following factors: if the person has the ability to do the role, if the person has motivation to do the role, and if the person fits well with the existing staff. Too many times, people are hired just on the basis of their resume. Just because someone has the right skills doesn't mean that they will want to do the role which has been designed by someone else. This is why it is critical during the interviewing process to understand whether the candidate is motivated to do the work he or she is applying for. Equally important is to understand if the candidate will fit in well with the existing staff. This includes personality, work style, and background. The Best Manager knows that hiring the right person is important not only for getting the job done, but also for helping the existing team to be more productive.

Who is responsible for employee's success?

This might surprise you, but it is not only employee who is responsible for his or her success! Organizations are quick to take the credit when the new person does well, and they are equally quick to blame the employee when things don't work out. The success of the hired person depends on the whole system. For example, a demanding micro-manager will get less performance out of the same person who, instead, might be doing well enough working for a smarter manager. Most people don't wake up in the morning and decide that today would be a good day to fail at work. Most people arrive at work with hope, anticipation, and feeling that they will do their best, and that they will have a productive day. The Best Manager knows that the system, which a person works under, determines success. When things go wrong, The Best Manager will quickly examine the system to understand what failed. For example, let's say, a bank expects its customer service employees, who work at the desks in the main customer waiting area, to open at least 5 new accounts per day. This bank decides to punish one employee who consistently for a week was opening only 1 account per day. The employee is upset; especially, knowing that there were other factors involved. The Best Manager would examine the system to see what is wrong. Upon investigation, the Best Manager would find out that many factors may have led to a poor week. The bank's credibility may have been impacted by an article in a newspaper, which was describing some ethical issues in the bank's operations. Or a new bank just opened down the block and was offering free iPods to any new customer, for opening an account. The Best Manager would involve the staff to see what new ideas and plans should be put into a place. There is no blame to pass around.

How to measure new hire assimilation

Most of the time, there is little formal measurement done to determine whether the new employee is fitting in. The Best Manager knows that the best way to measure is asking a new person on a regular basis how things are going, if a person is happy with the work, if objectives are clear for the person.

The Best Manager wants to know what a new employee needs in order to succeed. The Best Manager reviews the system and tries to understand whether it is supporting the new employee, and if he or she has good relationships with the peers. The Best Manager might look at whether the full potential of a new employee was used. The Best Manager will actually ask if the role is meeting his or her expectations. While these measurements are subjective, the important factor is that it involves both parties in the assessment.

What to do if things don't work out

Of course there will be times when things don't work. Many organizations move quickly to fire the employee. This should always be the last resort. Firing a person has many negative effects on the organization. First, morale suffers with those employees who remain. Second, many times this same function will be rehired within a year at 2-3 times of the cost. The Best Manager, instead, tries to understand what went wrong, and if it can be fixed. If not, then a two-way conversation takes place for working out a plan. This plan might involve retraining, it might involve a job rotation, or it might involve a period of time where the employee is given time to interview and pursue other opportunities in the organization. The organization gives these people top priority. Sadly, many organizations, instead, use this redeployment pool as a quick step towards abandonment and termination.

How to let go in a humanistic way

There will be times when people do need to be let go. It is very important how this occurs. Many organizations call outplacement firms to handle this process. An employee comes to work in the morning and meets a stranger. Then, 60 minutes later, someone else is cleaning up the office and bringing the employee's personal items to the parking lot. Many people are treated as criminals while letting them go. The Best Manager meets personally with the person impacted and answers all questions after discussing the reasons why the person is being dismissed. The Best Manager explains the next steps which include outplacement assistance for a fairly long period of time over many months to help the person find new work. The Best Manager knows this will help the credibility of the organization. When people are terminated in inhumane ways, the existing employees hear about this. Instead of doing their work, they will worry if they are going to be next. As a result, they work in fear and in reactionary mode. When people are let go in humanistic ways, existing employees know at least if things don't work out, they will have support in finding something else. The Best Manager knows that this is the right approach for a person and for the society.

Learning summary and next steps

It is important to understand that it is the system that determines the behavior and performance of its members. What is the process in your organization for hiring, evaluating, and letting go? Does it make sense? What parts need change and why? Only by asking these questions, the organization will have a healthy system where people want to work.

USING TIME WISELY BEFORE IT USES YOU

Do these time management habits sound familiar?

It is always interesting to me to observe how others especially managers manage their time. For example, when I was young in my career, I can remember one manager, who had a habit of trying to handle 3 things at once. I would be in his office trying to carry on a conversation and he would pretend to listen as he shouted another direction to his assistant and answered his phone at the same time. Another manager used to get up out of his chair at exactly the same time each night to leave. I was in my 20's and this was my first big job. My peers and I never would go home until the boss went home. He was about 6 feet 8 inches, and every night, when he was leaving, he would look over each cubicle to say goodbye. He was not the most organized manager. His desk was covered with pink message slips (this was before voicemail and e-mail) and you could barely tell what color his desk was. One night, when he was leaving, he looked over my cubicle wall and saw me sitting there with one piece of paper. I always preferred a clear desk and liked to work on one thing at a time. He stopped and said, "It looks like we need to give you more to do" and he left. More work! This was the last thing I wanted. So I got this idea. The next night, just before he was going to leave, I took my garbage can, which was filled with the papers, coffee cups, and other stuff from the day. I dumped it all on my desk. As my boss looked over the cubicle, he stopped this time and said, "Wow, it looks like you had a productive day!" I think I kept this process going for a few weeks just to show I was busy! Some managers still confuse activity with being productive! I had another manager, who although was at work all day, but it seemed he didn't get going until around 4 p.m. Sure enough, each day around 4 p.m., he came walking down the hall wanting to meet everyone and give each person more work! We usually did everything we could to avoid him at this time of the day. Some managers think that everyone else works the same ways they do!

The most common time-management mistakes

I have found in my career that people will tend to do what they like and what they are good at. I have also observed that people do things which are easy and don't take much time. I have seen many managers who respond well to crises and emergencies. I have had my fair share of managers who seemed to wait until the very last minute to plan anything! It seemed for these managers only a deadline worked for forcing some work to get done. It always amazed me, how many people work based on the first in and first out principle. These people just work on things based on the order of arrival! Finally, the most common management mistake, which I have observed, is that a person will work on demands from others and someone else's priorities vs. what was planned for the day.

What is time management?

We all have the same amount of time each day – 24 hours. The difference is how we use this time. Time management means to be aware of several factors. From a management perspective, it is always being aware of your own short- and long-term priorities, daily capacity, and how to leverage your own time. In management, each day is a challenge, and it seems like there is never enough time. Time management is exactly what it sounds like. Managing your own time vs. allowing time to manage you!

How does The Best Manager use time?

The Best Manager takes time to plan daily. The daily tasks are taken from a master list, which is a reflection of a greater strategy or plan. The Best Manager is careful not to schedule more personal work than his or her daily capacity is. It is important to carry a list and focus on deciding the result of which activities that day will return the most leverage. It means that you need to focus on achievements vs. what you would like to do. The Best Manager doesn't allow for interruptions (e-mail, phone, or small talk) when working on A priorities. Having a place for everything is also important. The Best Manager does one thing at a time, but several trivial things simultaneously. Make use of those extra few minutes while waiting for other activities to clear things off the list. Work on the most important items during your peak times of the day. The Best Manager doesn't procrastinate and keeps track of time always! It is important to always set deadlines as this helps one to prioritize daily. The Best Manager doesn't have time to worry; the more, worrying is not a good use of your time! The Best Manager schedules personal time to relax. Finally, using a system is helpful to keep yourself organized and it is more important to use a system that one feels comfortable with.

How to teach and demonstrate great time-management methods

I used to hold meetings late in the day and sometimes standing up! This gives a greater sense of urgency to the meeting as people want to finish and go home. Set a time limit for meetings and ensure that people know their role at meetings. This helps to reinforce good time management principles. Just following simple practices like being careful not to over schedule the day and learning to delegate can help one to keep on top of the most important tasks. Finally, I have learned over the years not to let papers sit around. Learn to handle paper once reviewing, and then either throw it away, file it, or take action. Many successful time managers use this philosophy.

Educating the workforce on time management

Invest time to teach people how to keep their workplace neat, organized, and free of clutter. Reinforce the importance of daily planning and following up. Prioritization is a great strategy to get the most leverage out of one's day. Teach people to use a system to plan, organize, and carry out their tasks daily. These are lessons which will last a lifetime.

The magic of time on your side in management

While we all have a certain amount of time each day, the Best Managers know how to move time over to their side. As a result, the most important things get done, and it seems like there is plenty of time left.

Learning summary and next steps

What system do you use to manage your time? How does the culture where you work behave with regards to time management? What could be improved? What do you need to do more of to manage your time better? What should you do less of? What small steps could you take today to become a better manager of your time?

MAKING MEETINGS REALLY WORK

Do you look forward to your next meeting?

If your answer is no, this does not surprise me. In over 25 years of managing, I saw many meetings which didn't work. Either the wrong people were there to make a decision or the right people were there, but the meeting leader was disorganized. Many times, the meeting was unstructured, and, as a result, it went over the time limit with little accomplished. Many times, there was not set any agenda, and it wasn't clear what the desired outcome of the meeting was. Many meetings which I attended didn't have a process to enable all participants to contribute, and, as a result, people shut down and didn't participate. I would just calculate the average hourly salary of each person in the room just to estimate how much time and money was wasted. Once I calculated that a meeting with 10 senior managers and human resources to make a decision on which type of coffee to have in the break room cost over three thousand dollars. It turned out that we couldn't agree and ended up meeting again!

Why many meetings are a waste of time

Many meeting leaders are confused which process to use for their meetings. For example, meetings where you want lots of open feedback and collaboration (mission meetings) led in an autocratic way with the only communication from the leader.

And opposite, normal staff meetings (where you want rigor and process) ran in an open, unstructured way, with everyone talking at once. No wonder why the staff never looks forward to coming to the meetings. At these organizations, people look at meetings as an interruption to their work!

How to make meetings work

There are simple steps to take in order to make meetings work. It takes discipline. First, decide if you are going to have a mission or a process meeting. Mission meetings are good to have if you need to solve a problem or create a new solution. In mission meetings, you want lots of collaboration, brainstorming, and less control from the leader. Process meetings are better suited for routine business meetings. The best example of a process meeting would be a routine staff meeting or frequent operational meeting. In these meetings, routine information is passed down. In these meetings, you want a leader who is rigor and in control. Normally, process meetings don't require open discussions.

Next, invite the right people to the meetings. Don't just invite the whole staff as many managers as you can. Invite only those people who have content to contribute, who are involved in making a decision, or who have tasks which are due for the meeting. Ensure that each person knows why he or she is invited.

Prepare an agenda. Having stated agenda timeframes is very important. I have observed that when timeframes are listed on the agenda for various topics, the group will work hard to enforce the guidelines. Stay on schedule! The worst habit a meeting leader can have is to start late and finish late. Issuing a task on the meeting, the leader must assign a responsible person and a date on when the task is due. It is good also to review these tasks at the end of the meeting, so everyone in attendance knows what is expected next.

In most meetings there is always one person who seems to bring up topics which have nothing to do with the stated agenda and takes everyone off track. Strong meeting leaders know how to handle this. As soon as the irrelevant topic comes up, the leader makes it clear that this might be an important topic to discuss but at a later date. The leader, however, respectfully takes the topic and writes it down on a flip chart labeled, for example, "Parking Lot". The person who brought it up feels better and everyone else in the meeting feels relieved that the meeting can continue on schedule!

Finally, it is important to publish written record of the meeting. These meeting minutes should be so clear that anyone who reads it, even without attending the meeting, would understand what was accomplished. The meeting minutes should include who attended, who was absent, and key decisions which were made. Additionally, the meeting minutes should include next steps, the responsible people of key tasks, and when these tasks are due. All this should be reviewed at the start of the next meeting. The meeting minutes should include details of when the next meeting is going to be, where it will be held, and what the related details are. Each meeting agenda should also state upfront the expected outcome. If there is no problem to be solved, no solution to be created, or no information to be passed down and discussed, there should not be a meeting!

The importance of follow up

Following up after each meeting is important and a key responsibility of the meeting leader. The leader should follow up on task progress, open issues which come up during the meeting, and provide guidance and direction as needed. The worst meetings are the ones which are run well but nothing happens after them. As a result, the company loses more time and productivity.

The organizational impact of good meetings

The Best Manager knows that efficient meetings save money, generate positive teamwork, and most importantly help to get things done. As a result, the organization builds good meeting processes into its culture and doesn't tolerate meetings which waste time and energy.

Learning summary and next steps

How do people where you work run meetings, and what could be improved? What processes are used to organize and run meetings? Are they efficient? Why? Why not? What are three steps you can take to improve the culture of meetings in your office?

DEFEATING STRESS AT WORK

What causes stress at work?

Stress impacts all of us. It causes health problems and accidents and affects the national economy. In my management career, I observed that incompetent managers cause stress for their employees. These managers seem to always adopt a crisis mindset when managing. They rarely listen to others; they lack creativity and rely on old habits. Their approaches cause stress for people they manage. Incompetent managers give unclear directions, apply unrealistic expectations, and micro-manage their employees. All of this causes stress for people. At the same time, people bring stress from home. This mix of personal concerns, poor management, and constant pressure to perform to external expectations at work can cause much stress.

When stress is bad

Stress is bad when expectations are not clear at work and people are confused about what they are supposed to do. When people have challenging work and they don't have the right skills, it leads to burn-out and stress. When one is not challenged at work and has skills, which are not being used, it can lead to boredom and then stress as a result. Stress is bad when a person has inadequate coping methods for dealing with the stress. Some people react to stress with increased anxiety and openly show their anger. Others resist things and get suppressed. Another group of people give in easily and finally give up. All these approaches are not healthy. People cause their own stress. Initially, generated thoughts of doubt and fears cause anxiety. Those who don't know how to deal with it experience stress as a chronic state. Work related and personal events can raise the potential of stress, but the reaction of every person to stress is very different.

What influences the way we react to stress?

There are many factors which will determine how we react to stress. Most of our reactions are learned behavior. The ways we condition ourselves will have a big impact on the way we react to stress. For example, one person might notice that the manager didn't smile or say hello in the morning. By the evening this person will cancel the family vacation, child's dental braces, and a new coat as a result of being convinced to be fired soon. Another person in the same situation might think spending less than a few seconds on this, "Oh, I guess the boss has some problems."

Money pressures, health pressures, lack of joy at work, lack of confidence, relationship issues, all that can lead to stress at work. Again, how we react is what is most important.

How to manage stress in the best way

Individuals can actually manage and even defeat stress through multiple strategies. For example, adopting an internal locus of control can defeat stress. Learning to control your own thoughts and behaviors from within can defeat the habit of always overreacting to external events, opinions, and behavior. Having great health resiliency can help to defeat stress too. This can include to sleep well, to eat healthy, and to get lots of exercise. Being in a great shape can make a person feel so good, so strong, and full of energy that even having the most negative person around can't be a problem. Finally, having a strong social network can reduce the possibility for stress. Having close friends, peers, and positive social network can help to reduce stress. You will often notice that The Best Manager usually has a strong social network.

It is also important just to measure and be aware of your own stress levels. Start to become aware when you are more tired, confused, upset, and distracted. This is the time when you will need to use your stress defeating strategies. The art of reframing can help one to reduce stress. For example, when experiencing a stressful situation, you can ask yourself, "Do you realize that... (*Think of a positive answer to the question which can reduce your stress*)?" I like these sorts of questions, "Isn't it great that..." and "I am grateful for...." This reframing causes your mind to refocus from the negative thoughts reducing the influence of the external event and instead focus on an internally generated question and event.

Most of the time these external events can trigger stress but remember it's the meaning we place on the words or events which can cause the stress! Of course many stressful events will not go away especially at work. A person of greater resiliency has a better position for defeating the negative effects of stress.

The Best Managers take good care of themselves. They balance their life, build physical and psychological resiliency, and learn to relax more. The Best Managers learn to trigger thoughts and behavior from the inside out while maintaining a strong social network.

Stress will always be present, but how we deal with it will determine how we feel and react to it.

Learning summary and next steps

Identify the factors which cause you the most stress at work. Make a second list and identify what you can do to reduce and/or defeat the stress. Think through how these factors might affect others, who you lead. Identify specific internal things you can do to defeat the stress. Recognize your physical, emotional, and mental responses which would defeat and or reduce the most stressful elements that you experience at work.

PEOPLE DIFFERENCES AND THE EFFECT ON BEHAVIOR AT WORK

Wouldn't it be great if we all got along well?

Have you ever met people at work with whom you really got along well? Have you ever met people at work with whom you wished you would never meet again? What causes these great differences? Too often, we are expecting others to be just like us. When they fail to meet our expectation, we decide we don't like to work with them. It would be so much easier if people with whom we work all behaved the same. It would be easier if they listened to what we wanted to tell them, acted in the ways we expected, and thought about things in the same ways we did. It would be easier, but it will never happen.

How are we different?

Our backgrounds, which include how, where, and when we were raised, play an important part in our differences. Our experiences play a big part. Our economic backgrounds play a difference. Our wired personalities from birth play a difference. Our beliefs and values play a difference. When we come to work, we bring many desires, concerns, and challenges from home with us. As a result, the expectations we bring to work are large and many times are not possible to be met from the workplace. This can lead to many conflict situations.

The best way to understand others

The Best Manager understands that people are different and knows that the best way to understand others is to become more self-aware. This starts with a curiosity around understanding others in order to develop insight into our own behavior. The deeper insight we have about ourselves, the more effective interactions we will have with others. This takes work and is a lifelong process. The ability to get along with others will impact one's career more than anything else. This starts with a healthy self-concept which determines one's behavior. When we understand ourselves and are at peace with ourselves, we have greater patience and understanding for others. At work, it has been my observation that many people have not taken time to become more self-aware. They wear masks at work, which may not reveal who they really are and how they feel about themselves. I have observed that people become defensive or protective when discussing personal information. As a result, for these people their relationships with others are shallow and superficial. This gets in the way when seeking positive working relationships at work. To enable yourself to be not so sensitive, it is important to self-monitor your behavior. It can be healthy to seek out objective information about your behavior from others who care. The more self-aware you become, the more tolerant you will be of others.

What does personality have to do with it?

Everything! So much of our behavior is affected by our core personality which stays with us most of our life. Personality is a complex combination of characteristics that include mental and physical attributes and determine our identity.

Personality is who we are and why we behave the way we do. Our personality is stable over time and across many different situations. For most people we develop our personality habits which drive our behavior. So many factors affect our core personality. As a result, at work these core attributes all seem to collide especially when trying to get things done with others. The Best Manager understands that helping people understand and appreciate the diversity between people is the best approach for healthy and productive relationships at work.

Emotions and behavior

When people get upset at work many times the anger or frustration is only triggered by one event but really is associated with another event. Sometimes we forget this. We make assumptions at work. We label people at work too often. We say this person has high potential and this person is slower than others. One person might be labeled too vocal and another person too timid. We forget that all of these emotions and behavior at work is part of our core personality and the way we view the world and others. Rather than trying to change people, The Best Manager knows it is better to have tolerance for ambiguity with others. This helps one to communicate better, be more adaptive and sensitive to other's characteristics. As a result of people differences, organizations develop their own personalities based on people they hired. This is why it is so critical to work in a culture which fits one's personality and values.

Implications for the Best Manager

The Best Manager knows that people are complex and their behavior is a combination of reactions based on how they think and what they have experienced in the world. The best strategy for developing people at work is to value the differences. The Best Manager understands that diversity increases creativity and innovation. It also increases conflict. The Best Manager knows that sometimes conflicts are helpful for finding the right solution and solving the problem. With greater self-awareness, we will accept who we are, work on those elements which need to develop, and accept that others are in different phases of their own self-development. Are there people differences at work? Yes! Do they impact behavior? Yes! The Best Manager accepts this as both the challenge and opportunity of leading others.

Learning summary and next steps

What educational opportunities can you put in place to enable people to understand and value the differences in others who they work with? How can you encourage a person to be a role model who values diversity in others? What processes can you put into place to educate the workforce on organizational values and behavior? Where are the challenges in your organization with regards to behavior and what could be done to bring greater self-awareness and people development tools to your organization? What are the top 3 challenges and developmental opportunities where you work with regards to people and their differences?

The Best Manager Self-assessment ©2010
Craig Nathanson

Leadership comes naturally to some of us, and not that easily to the rest of us. The good news is that anyone can learn and practice leadership skills. Development in this area will improve your outlook on life, help you accomplish your goals, and bring you success in your organizational life. Take this assessment based on Craig's original research to see where you stand now, and where you can develop to be The Best Manager!

Note: This assessment can be useful for those in leadership positions, those wanting to move into leadership positions, or anyone just wishing to develop leadership skills in themselves and others.

1.   I have a good sense of my values, and what is most important to me.

Strongly Disagree	Disagree	Don't Know	Agree	Strongly Agree
1	2	3	4	5

2.   I have spent time in reflection, and I have a sense of self-awareness.

Strongly Disagree	Disagree	Don't Know	Agree	Strongly Agree
1	2	3	4	5

3. I know how to persuade and influence others.

Strongly Disagree	Disagree	Don't Know	Agree	Strongly Agree
1	2	3	4	5

4. I know how to create and communicate a vision to others.

Strongly Disagree	Disagree	Don't Know	Agree	Strongly Agree
1	2	3	4	5

5. I know where I have personal mastery and passion related to my work.

Strongly Disagree	Disagree	Don't Know	Agree	Strongly Agree
1	2	3	4	5

6. I know how to create team learning.

Strongly Disagree	Disagree	Don't Know	Agree	Strongly Agree
1	2	3	4	5

7. I apply daily integrity in all my activities, and I have a good sense of what this means to me.

Strongly Disagree	Disagree	Don't Know	Agree	Strongly Agree
1	2	3	4	5

8. I understand the ideas around systemic thinking, and I am able to apply this in my daily decision-making process.

Strongly Disagree	Disagree	Don't Know	Agree	Strongly Agree
1	2	3	4	5

9. I am creative, and I know how to develop and apply creativity in my work.

Strongly Disagree	Disagree	Don't Know	Agree	Strongly Agree
1	2	3	4	5

10. I am decisive, and I make many decisions during the course of my day.

Strongly Disagree	Disagree	Don't Know	Agree	Strongly Agree
1	2	3	4	5

11. I tend to be outgoing, and those that I connect with find me charismatic.

Strongly Disagree	Disagree	Don't Know	Agree	Strongly Agree
1	2	3	4	5

12. I tend to achieve the goals which I set for myself and/or my team.

Strongly Disagree	Disagree	Don't Know	Agree	Strongly Agree
1	2	3	4	5

13. I apply proven time management principles and manage my time well.

Strongly Disagree	Disagree	Don't Know	Agree	Strongly Agree
1	2	3	4	5

14. I am constantly seeking to develop and improve my skills.

Strongly Disagree	Disagree	Don't Know	Agree	Strongly Agree
1	2	3	4	5

15. I treat others exactly how I wish to be treated.

Strongly Disagree	Disagree	Don't Know	Agree	Strongly Agree
1	2	3	4	5

16. I am an excellent communicator.

Strongly Disagree	Disagree	Don't Know	Agree	Strongly Agree
1	2	3	4	5

17. I know how to celebrate my accomplishments and the accomplishments of others.

Strongly Disagree	Disagree	Don't Know	Agree	Strongly Agree
1	2	3	4	5

18. I know how to build and develop strong teams.

Strongly Disagree	Disagree	Don't Know	Agree	Strongly Agree
1	2	3	4	5

19. I have perfect writing skills, and I know how to communicate my ideas in writing.

Strongly Disagree	Disagree	Don't Know	Agree	Strongly Agree
1	2	3	4	5

20. I always make others and their work important to me.

Strongly Disagree	Disagree	Don't Know	Agree	Strongly Agree
1	2	3	4	5

21. I place more emphasis on giving feedback than evaluation to those who I manage.

Strongly Disagree	Disagree	Don't Know	Agree	Strongly Agree
1	2	3	4	5

22. I place emphasis on collaboration vs. competition with those who I manage.

Strongly Disagree	Disagree	Don't Know	Agree	Strongly Agree
1	2	3	4	5

23. I teach my staff how to develop internal motivation.

Strongly Disagree	Disagree	Don't Know	Agree	Strongly Agree
1	2	3	4	5

24. I am aware of the differences between coaching and managing

Strongly Disagree	Disagree	Don't Know	Agree	Strongly Agree
1	2	3	4	5

25. I am aware of the differences between leading and managing.

Strongly Disagree	Disagree	Don't Know	Agree	Strongly Agree
1	2	3	4	5

26. I involve my staff in the annual planning process.

Strongly Disagree	Disagree	Don't Know	Agree	Strongly Agree
1	2	3	4	5

27. I communicate on a regular basis with those who I manage.

Strongly Disagree	Disagree	Don't Know	Agree	Strongly Agree
1	2	3	4	5

28. I discuss and demonstrate to my staff what quality means.

Strongly Disagree	Disagree	Don't Know	Agree	Strongly Agree
1	2	3	4	5

29. I work with each staff member on development plans which align to their work related goals.

Strongly Disagree	Disagree	Don't Know	Agree	Strongly Agree
1	2	3	4	5

30. I work with staff on alternative solutions when things don't work out before simply laying- off.

Strongly Disagree	Disagree	Don't Know	Agree	Strongly Agree
1	2	3	4	5

31. I practice good meeting management discipline and process.

Strongly Disagree	Disagree	Don't Know	Agree	Strongly Agree
1	2	3	4	5

32. I understand the differences among people and use this knowledge to help people to work together.

Strongly Disagree	Disagree	Don't Know	Agree	Strongly Agree
1	2	3	4	5

33. I share all financial news and updates with my staff.

Strongly Disagree	Disagree	Don't Know	Agree	Strongly Agree
1	2	3	4	5

34. I share all customer updates and business plans with my staff.

Strongly Disagree	Disagree	Don't Know	Agree	Strongly Agree
1	2	3	4	5

35. I treat each person as unique and special.

Strongly Disagree	Disagree	Don't Know	Agree	Strongly Agree
1	2	3	4	5

36. I don't use reward and punishment as a management tactic.

Strongly Disagree	Disagree	Don't Know	Agree	Strongly Agree
1	2	3	4	5

37. I help my employees to align their abilities and interests.

Strongly Disagree	Disagree	Don't Know	Agree	Strongly Agree
1	2	3	4	5

38. I practice daily how to defeat the stress which comes up at work.

Strongly Disagree	Disagree	Don't Know	Agree	Strongly Agree
1	2	3	4	5

39. I eat well, sleep well and exercise on a daily basis.

Strongly Disagree	Disagree	Don't Know	Agree	Strongly Agree
1	2	3	4	5

40. I help my employees find joy and passion in their work.

Strongly Disagree	Disagree	Don't Know	Agree	Strongly Agree
1	2	3	4	5

HOW DID YOU SCORE?

160-200 = A   Your leadership skills make you a role model of the Best Manager. You lead yourself and others in a systematic way. You have a strong sense of yourself and others. Your communication and interpersonal skills are strong. You have a deep interest in developing yourself, and you are interested in others and their development.

120-159 = B   You have many qualities of the Best Manager with strong self-leadership and leadership of others. You know how to motivate yourself and you have a good understanding of others. Although some gaps do exist, you are a fairly strong leader. Focusing on the areas that you don't generally practice will benefit you as a leader.

80-120 = C   You have significant gaps towards becoming the Best Manager based on your self-leadership traits and in leading others. Addressing these gaps will enable you to achieve your personal and work-related goals. Work on one area at a time and focus on practice and developmental opportunities. Over time, you can acquire the skills needed for self-leadership and leadership of others. A strong focus on leading from a systemic view will benefit you.

< 80 = D   You are not yet the Best Manager. Your leadership of yourself and others tends to be very reactive, and stems from a non-systemic view. This approach can severely impact your progress toward personal and organizational goals. A new approach is needed now. Lots of practice, developmental opportunities, and reflection will assist in making this change to stronger self-leadership and leadership of others.

Craig's biography

Craig Nathanson has 28 years of experience at the senior levels in both technology and human resource related areas (Intel, Amdahl, and Right Management Consultants). Mr. Nathanson was among the group of founders of Pandesic, one of the early e-commerce firms where he also was Director of Web-development as well as the Vice-President of PeoplePC, a joint venture with Ford Motor Company. His teaching experience is focused on management, human resources, and organizational behavior with many U.S. universities and colleges. Mr. Nathanson has been a visiting lecturer for the Academy of National Economy in Moscow, Russia; The Shenyang University of Technology, China; and National University of Vietnam, Vietnam. Craig has published three books including *P is for Perfect: Your Perfect Vocational Day* and in 2010 *How to Find the RIGHT Work during Challenging Times: A new approach to your life and work after 40.*

His online communities can be found at
www.thevocationalcoach.com and
www.thebestmanager.com .

He has been professionally affiliated with American Society of University Professors, American Management Association, Association of Humanistic Psychology, and Association of Small Book Publishers. In the past, he was Vice-President Career Counseling and faculty Board Advisor at St. James Business College. Mr. Nathanson is a successful instructor and workshop leader and has a private practice where he works with adults over 40 with regards to their work. Additionally, Mr. Nathanson is active as an executive coach and workshop leader on management practices for organizations and a keynote speaker. Mr. Nathanson earned his M.A. in Human Development from the Fielding Graduate Institute, California. He received his M.S. in Telecommunications Management from Golden Gate University, California and B.A. in Human Relations and Organizational Behavior at University of San Francisco, California. Mr. Nathanson was doing his Ph.D. research in Human and Organizational Development at The Fielding Graduate Institute, California. Craig lives with his family in Petaluma, California.

References

Argyle, M. (1989). *The Social Psychology of Work: Revised Edition* (2nd ed.). Boston: Penguin (Non-Classics).

Barker, J. A. (1993). *Paradigms: The Business of Discovering the Future*. New York: Harperbusiness.

Benjamin., & Franklin, 1. (1994). *The Autobiography of Benjamin Franklin*. Boston: Public Domain Books.

Bridges, W. (2009). *Managing Transitions: Making the Most of Change* (Third Edition). Cambridge: Da Capo Lifelong Books.

Brodow, E. (2004). *Beating the Success Trap: Negotiating for the Life You Really Want and the Rewards You Deserve*. New York: Harper.

Cialdini, R. B. (2007). *Influence: The Psychology of Persuasion (Collins Business Essentials)*. London: Collins.

Csikszent, M. (2007). *Flow: The Psychology of Optimal Experience (P.S.)*. New York: Harper Perennial Modern Classics.

Csikszentmihalyi, M. (1994). *The Evolving Self*. New York: Harper Perennial. (Original work published 1993)

Csikszentmihalyi, M., Damon, W., & Gardner, H. (2001). *Good Work: When Excellence and Ethics Meet*. New York: Basic Books.

Deci, E., Flaste, R. (1996). *Why We Do What We Do. Understanding Self-Motivation:* New York: Penguin.

Deming, W. E. (2000). *Out of the Crisis*. London: The Mit Press.

Drucker, P. F. (1994). *Management* (New ed.). Oxford: Butterworth-Heinemann Ltd.

Drucker, P. F. (2006). *The Practice of Management* (Reissue ed.). London: Collins.

Ed.D, Holton, E. F, Iii, Knowles, M. S., Ph.D., Ph.D., et al. (2005). *The Adult Learner, Sixth Edition: The Definitive Classic in Adult Education and Human Resource Development* (6 ed.). St. Louis: Butterworth-Heinemann.

Fritz, R. (1994). *The Path of Least Resistance*. Oxford: Butterworth-Heinemann Ltd.

Gardner, H. E. (1993). *Frames Of Mind: The Theory Of Multiple Intelligences* (10th ed.). New York: Basic Books.

Gendlin, E. T. (2007). *Focusing*. United States and Canada: Bantam.

Handy, C. (1998). *The Age of Unreason* (1st ed.). New York: Harvard Business School Press.

Handy, C. (1999). *The Hungry Spirit*. New York City: Broadway. (Original work published 1998)

Herrmann, N. (1989). *The Creative Brain* (Revised ed.). Lake Lure, : Ned Herrmann Group, The.

Hollis, J. (2000). *Creating a Life: Finding Your Individual Path*. Toronto: Inner City Books.

James, W. (2009). *THE PRINCIPLES OF PSYCHOLOGY*. New York: Classics-Unbound.

Kohn, A. (1992). *No Contest: The Case Against Competition* (Rev Sub ed.). New York: Mariner Books.

Kuhn, T. S. (1979). *The Essential Tension: Selected Studies in Scientific Tradition and Change* (New ed.). Chicago: University Of Chicago Press.

Nathanson, C. (2003). *P Is For Perfect: Your Perfect Vocational Day*. Danville: Book Coach Press.

Nathanson, C. (2010). *How to Find the RIGHT Work for Challenging Times*. Petaluma, : Lulu.com.

Oech, R. v. (2008). *A Whack on the Side of the Head: How You Can Be More Creative* (25 Anv. Rev ed.). unknown: Business Plus.

Rose, C. P., & Rose, C. (1989). *Accelerated Learning*. New York: Dell.

Seligman, M. E. (2006). *Learned Optimism: How to Change Your Mind and Your Life*. New York: Vintage. (Original work published 1990)

Senge, P. M. (2006). *The Fifth Discipline: The Art & Practice of The Learning Organization*. New York: Currency.

Zinsser, W. K. (2006). *On Writing Well, 30th Anniversary Edition: The Classic Guide to Writing Nonfiction (On Writing Well)* (30 Anv. ed.). London: Collins.

Peters, T., & Jr, R. H. (1982). *In Search of Excellence Lessons from America's best Run Companies* (Presumed First Edition). New York: Harper & Row.